Loving Heart
Peaceful Mind

Rational Buddhism Workbook

M. Sekiyo Sullivan

ISBN-13: 978-1484846896
ISBN-10: 1484846893

DEDICATION

May all beings be free from animosity; may they live long, happy lives.
I dedicate any merit that arises from this publication to:
My teachers Than Chaokhun Phra Vijitrdhammapani,
Rev. Koyo S. Kubose and Ven. Khai Thien;
All beings in the Dharma worlds;
and all those in suffering and sorrow.
May penetrating light dispel the darkness of ignorance.
Let all karma be resolved and the mind-flower bloom in eternal spring.
May we ascend to the throne of liberation
and realize the enlightened way together.

CONTENTS

ACKNOWLEDGMENTS

This book would not have happened without a great deal of help from my teachers and mentors both on the Buddhist side and the secular side. There have been many, but I would particularly like to acknowledge Philip Tate, Ph.D., Debbie Joffe Ellis, Ph.D. and the late Albert Ellis, Ph.D. for the wisdom and encouragement each imparted along the way.

I dedicated merits from this work to my teachers Ven. Khai Thien, Rev. Koyo Kubose and Than Chaokhun Sunan Phra Vijitrdhammapani, because if I have accrued any merit through my practice, it is because of their great kindness and guidance.

My wife, Michelle Jouyo Sullivan, is a constant source of inspiration and encouragement, and her support during the creation of this publication has been and continues to be invaluable.

Without great students, there would be no great teachers. If I have attained any usefulness as a dharma teacher, it is because I have had such wonderful students.

I hope this work helps you expand your understanding of the Buddhist path and how training your mind can lead to happier, more enlightened living. May I be forgiven any misstatements and omissions of the Dharma that appear due to my lack of realization.

1 RATIONALITY AND BUDDHISM

Every Thursday afternoon, about a dozen men convene in a makeshift meditation hall at a correctional institution near Daytona Beach. Beneath too-bright fluorescent lights and separated only by sliding vinyl walls from chatting chapel clerks on one side and a Jehovah's Witnesses meeting on the other, these Buddhist inmates meditate for 20 or 30 minutes and then discuss ways the dharma can help them cope with the realities of their lives.

During one such afternoon, a recovering drug addict doing time for offenses ranging from burglary to resisting arrest with violence asked me an interesting question. He has been practicing Buddhism for about five years and is also in a recovery program that incorporates Rational-Emotive Behavior Therapy (REBT). He wondered: Can he incorporate REBT into his Buddhist practice? And could his Buddhist practice enhance his understanding of REBT?

His question tapped into a train of thought I'd already spent quite some time pondering.

Albert Ellis, who introduced REBT in 1955, suggested therapists and their patients employ a simple but effective method, the "ABCs of REBT," to determine which cognitions are involved with stress and suffering and then work to eliminate or reduce their impact. Similarly, the Buddha's concept of Right Effort encourages the practitioner to examine the mind and determine if there are harmful or helpful mental states present, and then to abandon the harmful ones and cultivate the helpful ones. The two approaches easily go hand-in-hand, and REBT can help put sometimes difficult Buddhist ideas into a more down-to-earth, day-to-day perspective.

I first became interested in the idea of Rational Buddhism around 1990. At the time, I was practicing meditation with a Thich Nhat Hanh-inspired group while also leading meetings of an REBT-based self-support program for people recovering from alcohol and/or drug dependencies. I noticed a profound congruence between what practitioners of both REBT and Buddhism were doing.

While working under the mentorship of Philip Tate, Ph.D., a psychologist who had trained at the Institute for REBT in New York, I listened one day while a young woman described struggling with an eating disorder and problematic drinking habits along with what she called "self-esteem issues." Dr. Tate listened to her, and then answered compassionately, but directly: "Self-esteem is a sickness."

Hearing that statement, I felt as if someone had just handed me the answer key to a book of Zen koans. I had read about the Buddhist teaching of anatta—not-self—and more or less understood intellectually that what we see as "self" is really a changing set of processes conditioned upon other processes. However, this simple statement about the fallacy of self-esteem hit me right in the gut: From an ever-changing, amorphous set of processes, we create an illusion of a tangible self. We then rate or "esteem" that illusory self, potentially leading to very real day-to-day suffering including everything from panic attacks and depression to eating disorders, alcohol dependency and other afflictions.

During his career, Ellis had also noticed similarities between REBT and Buddhism. Ellis felt therapy should aim to help people suffer less and enjoy life more, and he had lauded the Buddha for recognizing that we can reduce suffering by learning better ways to use the mind.

After my conversation with the inmate mentioned above, I began suggesting to meditators they try adding what I've come to consider "The ABCs of Rational Buddhism" to their spiritual toolbox alongside traditional mindfulness and concentration practices. Often, people discover that rational analysis of their views and intentions helps them alleviate the anger, depression, anxiety and other emotional and behavioral difficulties they identify when they start practicing meditation.

This book is a continuation of that process. I have set an exploration of Ellis' process of examining and working with one's cognitions into the context of a very traditional Buddhist practice, the cultivation of the four Brahma-Viharas: goodwill, compassion, appreciation and equanimity.

The idea of merging the two came to me after an event at which I was one of a half-dozen speakers from different Buddhist traditions. During a panel discussion afterward, one person asked an interesting question. "Most of us aren't monks, and we have to fit our meditation practice into the rest of our lives, so we have limited time," he said. "Is there one practice you'd suggest that would give me the biggest bang for the buck—the most benefit for the time I can set aside for meditation?"

I have studied several different kinds of meditation and find different approaches very helpful, but I think that for people who have to work meditation practice into an already tight schedule, cultivating the Brahma-

Viharas is an excellent approach to meditation to enhance daily living. It doesn't require hours of endless concentration in order to be effective, is fairly easy to learn, and it yields tangible rewards fairly quickly.

The basis of our Brahma-Viharas practice will mainly follow guidelines set out in a 1,600-year-old document, Bhadantacariya Buddhaghosa's *Visuddhimagga*. However, to enhance our investigation, I will also introduce another "spiritual tool" from the extreme contemporary end of the continuum of Buddhist practice, a Japanese practice called Naikan, which I find helps many people expand their view of their world and their relationships.

ABCs of Rational Buddhism

Before we start meditating, let's take a preliminary look at how rationality might mesh with your Buddhist practice.

About 500 years BCE, the Buddha taught that our suffering is a consequence of our mental activity. That doesn't mean our suffering is "all in our mind"—it can definitely be in our bodies and behaviors, and it can be affected by the world we live in. However, without the engagement of the mind, there's no suffering.

The Buddha specifically attributed suffering (dukkha) to a handful of mental activities that are mainly cognitive in nature and that fall under the general heading of "ignorance." There's a doctrine among the Buddha's key teachings, Dependent Origination, in which the Buddha outlined the way ignorance leads to suffering.

Dependent Origination is a complex concept that works on a number of levels. For example, it's often used to explain how the kilesas—the "stains" ignorance leaves on consciousness—lead to rebirth. However, I hope to demystify it somewhat here by focusing on the relatively humanistic side of this process.

Here's the Buddha's teaching as it appears in the Pali Canon:

Avijjā-paccayā saṅkhārā,
With ignorance as a condition there are sankharas (mental formations).

Saṅkhāra-paccayā viññāṇaṃ,
With sankharas as a condition there is consciousness.

Viññāṇa-paccayā nāma-rūpaṃ,
With consciousness as a condition there are mind-and-body (nama-rupa).

Nāma-rūpa-paccayā saḷāyatanaṃ,
With mind-and-body as a condition there are the six senses.

Saḷāyatana-paccayā phasso,
With the six senses as a condition there is contact.

Phassa-paccayā vedanā,
With contact as a condition there is feeling.

Vedanā-paccayā taṇhā,
With feeling as a condition there is craving.

Taṇhā-paccayā upādānaṃ,
With craving as a condition there is clinging.

Upādāna-paccayā bhavo,
With clinging as a condition there is becoming.

Bhava-paccayā jāti,
With becoming as a condition there is birth.

Jāti-paccayā jara-maraṇaṃ soka-parideva-dukkha-domanassupāyāsā sambhavanti.
With birth as a condition, then aging, death, sorrow, lamentation, pain, distress, and despair come into play. (The Dhammayut Order in the United States of America, 1994)

I've illustrated this with a diagram:

The 12 Factors of Dependent Origination

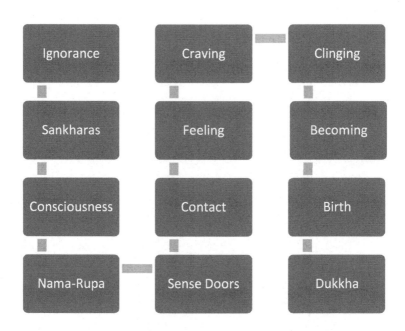

This probably seems confusing, and it might be hard to see at first what it has to do with your day-to-day life. However, this demonstrates how our experience of events comes equipped with baggage, including ignorance, which includes delusion or irrationality, and thus our reactions to those events are colored by that ignorance.

Things come into our awareness through Contact, which is what happens when our physical form (Rupa) and that which can be named but not seen (Nama) encounter one another. For instance, you might be sitting on your meditation cushion and develop an ache, which is a Feeling. That ache arises because of Contact, which you're aware of because of the Sense Door of touch.

The Sense Door is only there because Nama-Rupa (Mind-Body) is there, and that includes Consciousness. Consciousness comes equipped with Sankharas, which are mental processes. Some of those processes are rooted in Ignorance. Thus the Feeling, which is unpleasant, becomes an object of Craving (I *can't stand* this discomfort, perhaps), followed by a Clinging (I *need* to move). That leads to Becoming—becoming fidgety, maybe, or becoming doubtful that you can get any "good" out of this practice that's so intolerably uncomfortable.

So you experience "Birth" as a person who gives up on meditation rather than working harder to develop concentration and mindfulness. Thus you experience the Dukkha that you were hoping to transcend by learning to meditate.

Now let's fast-forward from 2500 BCE to the middle of the previous century, and talk about how to use Rational Buddhism to deal with Craving, Clinging, and Ignorance-Based Sankharas.

The ABCs of Rational Buddhism

The process of Rational Buddhism is based on the principles of Rational-Emotive Behavior Therapy, which was introduced in the 1950s by Albert Ellis, Ph.D., a psychotherapist who became disenchanted with traditional psychoanalysis and fathered what became the first of the cognitive therapies. Ellis summed up the practice of REBT in what he called "The ABC's of REBT," which we're going to co-opt for Rational Buddhism:

A. One perceives an activating event, activating experience or what we'll call an Adversity.

B. One's reaction to that event or experience is influenced by various Sankharas, including what we might call views or Beliefs. Those beliefs include both reality-based ones, which a Buddhist might call Right Views and which Ellis called Rational Beliefs (rB); and ignorance-based views, which Ellis calls Irrational Beliefs (iB).

C. Those Beliefs—both rational and irrational—lead to behavioral and emotional Consequences. Irrational, ignorance/delusion-based beliefs, lead to various forms of stress and suffering. (Ellis, 2001)

For example, when I'm walking my dog, I'll sometimes encounter a guy who walks his three dogs in some of the parks I visit. He never has his dogs leashed, and they have attacked mine a few times (no injuries, fortunately). When I tell him he is supposed to have his dogs leashed, he tells me to stop telling him what to do.

So, at (A), I have a run-in with the dog owner—that's the Adversity. At (C), I feel anger and other emotional Consequences; I also demonstrate behavioral Consequences, like yelling at him.

If you asked why I was angry, I might say it's because the guy doesn't leash his dogs—that (A) somehow causes (C). However, my anger and the other consequences are not caused by (A) as much as by the Beliefs (B) that I carry into that experience with me.

Those Beliefs include the rational thoughts that responsible pet owners obey leash laws and that it's unsafe and inconsiderate not to do so. If I stuck with those rational Beliefs, I wouldn't be "okay" with this dog owner walking his pets off the leash. I might point out patiently but firmly that he's breaking the law and creating a nuisance for which he could be fined and which could result in serious injury for his or someone else's dogs, to other people and possibly to himself.

Notice these rational Beliefs probably wouldn't be associated with a lack of emotion or to warm and fuzzy feelings, but to appropriately unpleasant emotions like annoyance and concern. Future encounters might lead to disappointment and frustration that the dog owner didn't heed my advice.

However, my rBs are accompanied by iBs—ignorance-based Sankharas/irrational Beliefs. In the Avijja Sutta, the Buddha defined ignorance as "the leader in the attainment of unskillful qualities." We might predict, then, that these irrational Beliefs, as Ellis explained, will not skillfully get me what I want but will unskillfully create hindrances.

My iBs might include the Belief this guy must or should be a responsible pet owner—that he should be concerned about the safety of others. I also irrationally believe that because he doesn't follow that rule and thus creates a problem for me, he's an arrogant bastard—which he shouldn't be—and that because I'm personally inconvenienced by his behavior, he deserves an ass-kicking. And when it happens again, I believe he must not be so dismissive of my well-intentioned advice and that pet owners like him should be easier to educate.

With those beliefs in operation, I might get Consequences like anger, yelling, low frustration tolerance, rage, obsessive thoughts of revenge or retaliation and maybe even physical assault—all over something that was over in less than a minute and with no actual harm done.

If I want to have a pleasant, relaxing walk outdoors with my dogs but instead spend much of the time obsessed with revenge fantasies, then my irrational Beliefs have hindered me in that effort. And if what I want is peace, serenity and happiness and instead I end up with rage, my ignorance has definitely led me to "the attainment of unskillful qualities."

Ellis catalogued many common irrational Beliefs, but we can summarize them in three main categories: First, there's the idea there's a "self" that can be rated—and thus either esteemed or damned—according to some subjective, often very narrow criteria. Second, we believe others *should* conform to our expectations, and that if they don't, they're *bad* or otherwise damnable people. Finally, we often believe environmental circumstances and conditions should support our own goals—the universe *should* give me what I *need* with little or no inconvenience to me.

The Buddha explained the problems with those ideas when he discussed concepts like not-self, karma, and dukkha. For example, in our practice, we come to understand the self to be an ongoing process of causes and conditions rather than a stable, discreet thing that can be rated. Ellis took a uniquely Buddhist point of view toward the idea of a self and the role the concept of self plays in creating our disturbances.

"Much of what we can call the human 'ego' is vague and indeterminate and, when conceived of and given a global rating, interferes with survival and happiness," he wrote. "People may well have their 'good' or 'bad' traits—characteristics that help or hinder them in their goals of survival and happiness—but they really have no 'self' that 'is' good or bad." (Ellis, 2001)

As for our expectations of others, if it were true that people "should" behave in a way that's best for everyone, we'd live in a world filled with fully enlightened bodhisattvas. Unfortunately, few people have the karmic foundation for that, and we all tend to repeat our mistakes. Anyone who has smoked more than one cigarette or gained weight during more than one holiday season can attest to that.

I can then evaluate the skillfulness of my views by Disputing—the (D) in the ABCs of REBT. Ellis suggested two ways of Disputing: examining the evidence for them or against them; and considering whether they are helpful or harmful, using these four questions:

(D) Disputing iB:

1.   Is there any evidence my belief is true?

2.   Is there any evidence my belief is false?

3.   What bad things might happen if I keep this belief?

4.   What good things might happen if I let go of this belief?

I might, for example, take a look at this belief: "Other dog owners must act perfectly responsibly; if he does not, he is a rotten person that deserves mistreatment, especially if he stupidly ignores my suggestion to behave differently."

If I look for evidence that statement is true or false, I will see that, while it certainly is better if dog owners act responsibly, that doesn't mean they *must* or even *should* do so. Understanding karma can help us with this one: We all live and act supported by our karma—some of us have the karmic foundation for that level of responsibility, and some of us do not.

So again, while I can talk until I'm blue in the face about how much better it would be if dog owners acted responsibly, any given individual dog owner will act according to his own set of causes and conditions. Yes, it might be stupid for him to ignore leash laws. Yes, it might be unsafe, and so on. But until his own karma brings him to that realization, he's probably not going to do any differently than he already does.

If I look with compassion at the dog owner, I will see the fallacy in the second part of the belief. The other dog owner's actions are the result of delusion and irrational thinking—like mine! I might even recall times I acted less than responsibly and even repeated the same mistake over and over. I don't think that proves I'm totally rotten, so it wouldn't apply to another pet owner.

When I ask what bad things will happen if I keep the belief, I see that hanging onto my belief could easily lead to more anger. I might even really lose my temper one day and punch the guy, which could land me in jail or earn me a lawsuit. However, if I give up the belief, I'll spend less time angry. With patience and restraint, I might even be able to get the guy to leash his dogs. If not, I can still enjoy more of my time outdoors with my own pets.

After Disputing my iBs about the dog owner, I can review the Effect of that process. More than likely, I'll reduce the anger I feel toward him, and I can work more calmly to deal with similar Adversities when they arise.

Have a look at the ABC Worksheet on the next page for an example of how I might analyze this using the ABCs of Rational Buddhism:

The ABCs of Rational Buddhism Worksheet

A. Adversity. Describe the event or experience that occurred. Avoid judging, labeling, etc.—simply describe the facts.

A guy often walks his dogs without leashes at the park, even after I've told him it's against the rules.

B. Beliefs. What beliefs do you have about this experience that get you upset, angry, disturbed, etc.?

He should pay attention to me and follow the rules, and since he doesn't, he's a total jerk.

C. Consequences. What emotions or behaviors did you experience because of your beliefs?

Anger; yelling at him; staying mad afterward and obsessing about him.

D. Disputing. Challenge your self-talk.

1. Is there any evidence my belief is true?

No. It would be better if he did, but there's no reason he "must" do what I think is best.

2. Is there any evidence my belief is false?

Yes—the best proof is that he doesn't pay attention to me and he doesn't follow the rules. People act according to their own causes and conditions, even if they do dumb, misguided things because of their karma. He probably thinks, albeit wrongly, that I'm a jerk for caring more about the rules than about his dogs. And he's obviously not a total jerk—he likes dogs a lot, so he can't be all bad.

3. What good might happen if I give up my belief?

I might get less angry; I might even be able to calmly help the guy understand the importance of complying with the leash rules.

4. What bad might happen if I keep my belief?

I might punch the guy; I'll keep getting angry and not enjoying our walks.

E. Effect. How have your feelings, behavior, etc. changed because of your disputing?

Less obsessing over the guy; I'm less likely to get really mad at him.

You will soon get the chance to try this process for yourself, using a situation where you experienced the arising of unskillful qualities in response to an adversity. It probably will not be quite as simple for you as that example. As I mentioned before, our thoughts and emotions when we are upset about something can be a tangled and complicated jumble of both rational and irrational ideas and both skillful and unskillful states of mind.

There are a few ways you can start bringing some order to that chaos. First, when you describe the (A) in the ABC, focus on what actually occurred, as if you were a video camera recording the event without interpreting it or judging it. Sorting out the actual fact of what happened from your feelings about it will help you identify which thoughts are perceptions of what happened and which are the processes you use to create stress.

For example, at one retreat, a woman said she had stopped going to the cafeteria at work because she was so upset about an "arrogant guy who's always in there" whenever she went to lunch. She was so upset about his rudeness she "couldn't stand to go there any more."

At first, we had some difficulty getting to the root of what she was even upset about. Once she focused on what actually happened, her (A) became, "A man I often see in the cafeteria doesn't say hello to me." Once she was able to see the event that clearly, it became much easier to distinguish between the activating event—the A in the ABC—and her feelings about it.

In this case, there were also a number of emotional consequences (C). When asked how she felt about it, her answer was "Very upset." We talked about that some more and narrowed that more specifically to anger, feelings of low self-esteem and anxiety.

Each of those consequent emotions will have a different belief associated with it. I asked if one of those was more significant or a bigger problem than the others; she said the anger outweighed the rest, so we focused on that.

When I asked, "Why do you feel angry at him?" the answer contained a very clear iB: "He should be polite and say hello to me."

Once she realized that belief was causing all that anger, she actually found it very easy to dispute (D): There were any number of reasons he might not say hello to her—including the reality that he might have rude, antisocial tendencies—but he might also be lost in thought, be overwhelmed by dissatisfaction in his job, and so on. And while it would be nicer if he treated her politely, she could certainly stand it and him if he didn't.

Think about a time you got upset about something or an ongoing situation that you're stressing about, and see if you can analyze it using the worksheet on the next page.

The ABCs of Rational Buddhism Worksheet

A. Adversity. Describe the event or experience that occurred. Avoid judging, labeling, etc.—simply describe the facts.

B. Beliefs. What beliefs do you have about this experience that get you upset, angry, disturbed, etc.?

C. Consequences. What emotions or behaviors did you experience because of your beliefs?

D. Disputing. Challenge your self-talk.

    1. Is there any evidence my belief is true?

    2. Is there any evidence my belief is false?

    3. What good might happen if I give up my belief?

    4. What bad might happen if I keep my belief?

E. Effect. How have your feelings, behavior, etc. changed because of your disputing?

Sidebar: Albert Ellis, Ph.D. and Buddhism

Much of the impetus for this book and for the concept of Rational Buddhism came to me during a series of conversations and correspondences I had with Albert Ellis' wife, Dr. Debbie Joffe Ellis, after his death.

For much of his life, Ellis was almost as renowned for his outspoken atheism and non-theistic humanism as he was for his groundbreaking cognitive-behavioral therapies. However, he wasn't entirely anti-religious, and toward the end of his life, he became interested in Buddhism and fascinated with its compatibility with REBT.

When he died in 2007, he had been working on a book on the topic. The book was never completed, but he and his wife collaborated on workshops discussing Buddhism and REBT. Ellis even attended talks by the Dalai Lama, who blessed a silk scarf and sent it to him for his 90th birthday.

"Al accused me of being that terrible influence" that drew Ellis toward Buddhism, Joffe Ellis jokingly told me. She admits she may have put some Buddhist books "under his nose," but is quick to add that he tended to make up his own mind about such matters.

"In his last few years, people would ask him if he was becoming more spiritual," she says. "He'd say, 'Based on the evidence at hand, I'm still skeptical. But if to care for others and the world and to try to contribute to humanity in positive ways is spiritual, then you can call me spiritual.'"

"His feeling was 'If it's beneficial, use it,'" she adds. "And there were features of various schools (of Buddhism) that Al found very compatible with REBT."

Both Ellis and the Buddha agreed that while difficulties are a part of every life, one's attitude and views about those difficulties creates or exacerbates the suffering one experiences.

"The internal factor creates more suffering than the external event itself, usually," says Joffe Ellis. "Both Buddhism and REBT recognize that" and try to get people to reduce their suffering by changing the way they think about events that affect them.

"For example, Vipassana and REBT both encourage skeptically and healthily evaluating one's thinking," she says. "Both encourage the use of reason to choose beliefs that are most life-enhancing."

Ellis felt REBT and Buddhism were both humanistic and pragmatic, she adds. "Al said both were spiritual—but he liked to talk about rational spirituality," she says. "That means a person is not merely self-centered, but cognizant of the fact there are other humans around."

Both Buddhism and REBT encourage compassion for others, but also for oneself, she says. "Al would point out that Buddhism and REBT both teach unconditional self-acceptance and other-acceptance, which is one of the things that set REBT's approach apart" from other therapies.

The Buddha and Ellis both treated compassion as a choice that can be cultivated with work and persistence. "It's not enough to just decide to 'achieve compassion,'" she adds. "You have to really work at it."

Like the Buddha, Ellis encouraged practitioners to recognize that other people want more happiness and less suffering, and to honor that. "Sometimes you have to compromise," Joffe Ellis says. "Compromise includes compassion, and compassion includes compromise."

Despite a public demeanor that at times could appear curmudgeonly— and even profane—Ellis was himself highly compassionate, she says. During his final years, Ellis was ousted from the organization he founded, the Institute for REBT, in a very public controversy.

"Al was treated very badly by the board," Joffe Ellis says. "But he consistently would say 'I don't hate those people—I just hate what they're doing.' He had compassion for them, because he recognized they acted the way they acted because of the disturbed way they think."

"Living with him through his final years, I saw him in tremendous, torturing pain from his illnesses and saw the deep sadness at what was happening with the Institute," she says. "The beauty of that situation, though, is that I was able to see Al refuse to get embittered or experience rage. That's one of the many things I adored about him—he practiced what he preached."

"The other thing I saw, which is another principle of REBT, is that he would focus on what's still good," she says. That doesn't mean adopting a Pollyannaish, pop psychology 'always look on the bright side' mentality, however. "Some things in life really are shitty—unfair and unjust," she says. "But Al was all for humans being human and enjoying fully whatever they could get from the present moment."

Both the Buddha and Ellis told people to try their practices and see for themselves if it worked, rather than merely accepting it on faith. "Both REBT and Buddhism encourage discernment," Joffe Ellis says. "Both say, 'Check this out and see if it works for you.'"

Ellis did point out his disagreement with ideas that appear in some schools of Buddhism. For example, he remained skeptical of any form of spirituality that tried to transcend the here-and-now, Joffe Ellis says, including forms of Buddhism that devote excessive attention to concerns about future lives or focus on deity-like Bodhisattvas.

"He considered it a waste of time to invest energy contemplating what might be, rather than investing energy in making the present moment as fine as possible," she says. "He didn't say [rebirth] was horseshit, but it was too mystical" to be a basis for a philosophy of living in the present.

He also felt the arahant ideal was too perfectionist. He pointed out that people have strong social and biological tendencies that make it unrealistic to try to totally eliminate all mental impurities.

"He wasn't saying there's no way," Joffe Ellis says. "But he wanted people to accept that we're fallible. REBT says you'll do well to overcome some of your imperfections," she adds. "But you're great and worthy of admiration just for being the fallible human you are."

"So he'd say, 'Let's work our asses off to eliminate much of our suffering and increase our joy,'" she says. "Maybe that's not nirvana, but it is a better way to live."

2 MEDITATION AND MINDFULNESS

Many westerners come to Buddhism mainly to learn about meditation. While a few decades ago there were relatively few resources in America for people wanting to learn to meditate, today there is the opposite problem—there is so much information it's hard to find a solid starting point for a path that will lead where you want to go.

When you first start wading through the information available about meditation, you can quickly get very confused. There can seem to be countless ways to meditate, and much of the explanation available comes in a confusing jumble of terms involving ancient languages like Sanskrit or Pali or scientific and/or pseudo-scientific jargon. When you boil it down to the basics, however, Buddhist meditation isn't all that complicated. Just remember there are different tools for meditators, and different situations call for different methods.

The last three factors on the Eightfold Path—Right Effort, Right Mindfulness and Right Concentration—all deal with meditation. Thus meditation deals with three main areas: concentration (*samadhi*); mindfulness (*sati*); and what the Buddha called *bhavana*, or cultivation of helpful mental states.

When you start meditating, it's generally best to begin by working with concentration, which means focusing all your mental activity on a single object. In Buddhist meditation, there's always an object of meditation—a focus for your awareness. There are an infinite number of possible meditation objects, but the breath is among the most useful. Breath is always with you and it doesn't have any particular spiritual or religious significance. Also, once you begin concentrating on your breath, you'll find it gives you a lot of information about what's going on in your mind and body.

Practicing concentration leads to calmness or tranquility (*samatha*).

Meditation teachers often compare the troubled mind to a container of dirty water: As long as the water stays agitated, it remains cloudy; once the water is allowed to be still, all that dirt begins to settle. If you let your mind remain still long enough, even the finest specks of dust will settle to the bottom. If you "rest" your awareness on an object, such as the rise and fall of the breath, all that "dirt and dust" floating around in your mind can settle, and your mind will gradually become calmer.

Mindfulness means to be fully aware and fully in the present. So if you're concentrating on your breath, for example, and anger arises, you're aware of the anger. However, you don't go chasing after it—if you're perpetuating the anger, then you're not in this moment and in this place. Rather, you're in some other moment and some other place when the anger-related event occurred or in the future when you get to act out your hostility.

Practicing mindfulness leads to insight (*vipassana*). There are different insights available to you when you meditate. For example, if you're practicing mindfulness, you may notice that you feel angry about the guy next to you in the meditation hall, because his stomach won't stop rumbling. If you look at that closely, you notice the stomach isn't really distracting you at all—your mind went off to explore this rumbling stomach instead of staying with your breath.

Instead of perpetuating your anger, you simply examine the elements that make it up—the mental fabrications, the physical sensations that arise from it, and so on. In the process, you may learn you've built a big chunk of your "self" around the idea that other people should control their stomach rumblings so you can have a peaceful meditation retreat. If you look at this closely and mindfully, you can see the three main Buddhist teachings in this one episode: anicca (impermanence—of the stomach rumbles and of your fleeting meditative tranquility); anatta (not-self, as in the "self" you were going to protect against this distraction); and dukkha (unsatisfactoriness of impermanent, insubstantial existence.)

Concentration and mindfulness really go hand-in-hand, although some types of meditation emphasize mainly concentration while others mainly emphasize mindfulness. In either event, we use concentration and mindfulness to determine if there are harmful mental states present in our mind, and if so, we let them go.

That brings us to Right Effort, which means noticing if there are harmful mental states present in our minds and letting them go. It also means to see if there are helpful mental states present, and if not, to cultivate them. The third type of meditation, bhavana, incorporates both concentration and mindfulness but uses contemplation to actively cultivate certain states of mind, especially goodwill, compassion and serenity.

The Buddha called such mental states Brahma-Viharas, which means "divine abodes" or "sublime attitudes." I'll explain these in detail later, as most of the work we'll be doing in this book will deal with cultivating these states of mind.

While unskillful states of mind like anger, ill will and anxiety lead to stress for ourselves and others, the brahma-viharas lead to reduced stress and increased happiness. With mindfulness meditation, if you notice you have anger, for example, you might see how it causes you trouble and learn you can let go of it. However, if you also cultivate its "antidotes," goodwill and compassion, you both loosen anger's connection to you and increase your capacity for love and caring.

There are a few more things you should have in mind before you start trying to meditate. First, remember that the purpose of meditation is to train the mind. The Buddha sometimes talked about the "monkey mind," which wants to jump from one distraction to another. If you've ever had to leash-train a puppy, you know what that's like. You pull the puppy over, make it sit, and it immediately jumps up and runs to play. So you pull it over again, make it sit, and it runs off again. You do that again...and again...and again...and finally the puppy learns what "sit" means. The mind in meditation can be a lot like that puppy.

Whenever your mind strays from the meditation object, just patiently, compassionately bring it back. If you're meditating on the breath, don't try to push thoughts away or force them not to arise—just let it go and return to the breath, let it go and return to the breath, let it go and return to the breath.

Often, people expect meditation to be a peaceful, enjoyable experience and they're disappointed when they spend the allotted time struggling. It is nice when the mind settles down, becomes calm, and we rise feeling refreshed and relaxed. However, those relaxing meditations aren't necessarily the "best" ones—sometimes we get much more from a half-hour of struggling.

Also, people sometimes have interesting or profound experiences during meditation one day and then want or expect the same thing to happen the next. Don't go into your meditation session with any particular expectation. It's much better to go to the cushion determined to train your mind, and then take whatever happens as a teaching.

If you read a dozen books on meditation, you'll find a dozen different opinions on when, how often and how long to meditate. The truth is, everyone is different. Some people start with a few minutes per day and work up from there, while others learn how to meditate by going to retreats where they immediately begin spending most of the day meditating. I suggest trying different things and seeing what works for you.

For our purposes here, we're going to begin with a basic meditation on the breath. This meditation mainly emphasizes concentration, which will help you reach a basic level of mental and physical calmness.

Meditating on the breath will help you become aware of your physical reactions to the Brahma-Vihara practices we'll do later on—if anxiety, anger, etc. arise, you'll notice a change in your breathing. When the other work gets stressful, you can switch back to meditating on the breath, calming your breath until you calm your mind.

PRACTICE: Anapanasati Meditation

There is a recorded Anapanasati Meditation available for your use. Written instructions also follow.

For the next several days, work with the recorded meditation until you feel comfortable doing it on your own. You can also refer to the written instructions before you meditate. Once you have learned the basics, it is not essential to do this meditation exactly the same as it is provided here. However, most people seem to find following the seven steps helps anchor the awareness on the breath and makes achieving a basic level of concentration go more smoothly.

Seven-Step Anapanasati (Mindfulness of Breathing) Instructions

1. Find a comfortable posture and turn your awareness to your breath. Take several deep breaths—breathing with your diaphram, letting it expand first, until you fill your lungs completely, then let the breath flow out, emptying your lungs completely.

2. Experiment with breathing in long and out long, in short and out short. Be aware of how it feels to take deeper and shallower breaths.

3. Now stop controlling your breath. Continue to breathe, but at a normal rate. Stay with your breath, and begin noting each breath with an "anchor" word or phrase. One traditional anchor is the word "Buddho"—you think silently to yourself as you breathe in, "Bud-" and as you breathe out, "Dho." Rising/falling and in/out are also traditional anchors.

4. Explore the path your breath takes as it flows in and out. Rest your awareness on the in-breath at the nostrils for several breaths. Feel each breath flow in through your nostrils. Shift your awareness lower, feeling each breath pass your palate, where the sinuses empty toward your throat, then shift to the base of your throat, to your lungs, then your diaphragm. Feel your diaphragm rising, then contracting, beginning the air's flow outward. Feel your lungs emptying, the air passing up through your throat, past your palate, out your nostrils.

5. Explore your body with your breath. Stay with your breath, but let your awareness take your breath through your entire body. Start with the toes— rest your awareness there and notice any sensations as your breath flows in and out. Continue this up your foot, moving from point to point up your body, feeling each part of your body with your breath until you reach the

top of your head.

6. Now rest your awareness at the tip of your nose or your belly, wherever you feel the breath most distinctly. Just stay with your breath there.

7. Keep refining the breath, calming it, until the mind is still. Sit with open awareness until the breath and mind become one.

When preparing to leave meditation, take your time. You may want to sway gently before you open your eyes to feel yourself in your body. Rub your hands together to warm them, if you like, and press them gently over your face and eyes. Finally, bring your hands together in *Gassho*—the "prayer" position, also referred to as *Anjali* in some traditions—to symbolize Oneness; bow your head and touch your hands to your forehead acknowledging the wisdom of a clear mind.

Mindfulness and Rationality

Not long ago, someone forwarded me a link to a blog by a California psychologist who had concerns about the practice of mindfulness in psychotherapy. He had watched a video on the topic by Jon Kabat-Zinn, the developer of Mindfulness Based Stress Reduction (MBSR), and was confused and more than a little critical: Isn't mindfulness, he wondered, with its emphasis on nonjudgmental awareness of one's thoughts and emotions, really just "mind-less-ness?"

During a course I gave in Rational Buddhism about that time, a participant wondered if maybe I was off track with the idea of analyzing one's thinking. As a lifelong Buddhist, she had learned about mindfulness as a way to transcend and transform stress. "I don't believe you can 'think' your way out of emotions," she said. Wouldn't "judging" the rationality of her thoughts clash with the practice of mindfulness?

These two concerns highlight a problem, but the problem is not with mindfulness as a practice. Rather, the problem is one of context. If you look closely, you find that mindfulness and rationality go hand-in-hand. In fact, they're not only complementary—each is almost useless without the other.

Mindfulness as a practice entered the western vernacular with Vipassana meditation groups, the writings of teachers like Vietnamese Zen master Thich Nhat Hanh and Buddhist practitioners like Kabat-Zinn, who adapted it for secular applications. In Buddhism, however, mindfulness is only one part of an eightfold path of practice. The problem arises when we try to separate it from the rest of the practice.

When I describe mindfulness—or more accurately, Right Mindfulness— I describe it as being fully aware and fully in the present. In their MBSR workbook, Kabat-Zinn colleagues Bob Stahl, Ph.D. and Elisha Goldstein, Ph.D. call it "being fully aware of whatever is happening in the present moment, without filters or the lens of judgment." (Stahl, 2010)

Thich Nhat Hanh explains mindfulness as knowing what is going on within and around us, and touching deeply the present moment.

None of these definitions explain very well what mindfulness is, how to practice it or its potential benefits. As used in Buddhism, the word "mindfulness" is a translation of the Pali word sati, which means to remember or keep in mind. So if we're practicing mindfulness of breathing as a meditation, for example, we remember to keep our attention on our breath.

To practice Right Mindfulness isn't just to be aware—it is to use awareness to gain control over the mind. A good way to start, as MBSR teaches, is to be aware of what's happening without the filter of judgment.

However, it doesn't end with that. Eventually, we also need to evaluate whether our mental actions lead us toward living in harmony with our surroundings or toward causing difficulties for ourselves and others. We will also be compelled to make changes in our views and intentions, and then to remember—to be mindful—of how well we're maintaining control over the mind.

This does not contradict MBSR, Zen Buddhism or other mindfulness practices. However, a lot of people who read the books and start trying to practice mindfulness get to the part about bare attention to the present moment, and they get stuck there.

Right Mindfulness is a very important factor of the Buddhist path; the Buddha himself said the diligent practice of mindfulness was necessary to attain enlightenment. In Buddhism, however, as well as in its secular applications, mindfulness is the axle around which a lot of other activity revolves.

Consider the concept of Right Livelihood, for instance. Before you can practice Right Livelihood, you need the wisdom to know whether or not the way you make your living will lead to stress and suffering for yourself and others. You will then need to set your mind (concentrate) on living in a way that not only supports yourself and others who depend on you but that treats your surrounding community with compassion. You make an effort to create such a livelihood for yourself, and you continually, mindfully monitor your activities to make sure you're still living in a way that aligns with these values.

People like Kabat-Zinn and Thich Nhat Hanh know mindfulness works in context with other factors, and working with cognitions and behaviors accompany the practice of bare attention in both MBSR and Zen Buddhism. Neither would ultimately discount the value of examining one's thinking and the role it plays in creating stress and suffering.

In *Peace is Every Step*, Thich Nhat Hanh includes a cognitive process in his approach to dealing with unskillful emotions that arise during meditation. It is a five-step method: recognize the emotion; become one with it; calm it; release it; and look deeply into it. (Nhat Hanh, 1991)

The first step, recognition, means to notice the emotion with bare attention. To do that, you name it. Once you have recognized something as what it is—anger, anxiety, etc.—you have some control over it. You stop feeding it by focusing on the external or internal circumstance that activated it, and shift your awareness to the emotion itself.

The idea of becoming "one with it" sounds exotic and mystical, but it really means to accept it, and this is as much a rational process as a mindful one. Often, before we can deal more rationally with our stressors, we first need to un-stress about being stressed. We get anxious about our anxiety, get angry at ourselves for getting angry at someone else, or we simply try to shove our emotion into the dark, denying it all together. It's much better to accept that we are human and that emotions—including unpleasant and unskillful ones—come packaged in that karmic bundle.

Once we recognize it and accept it, we are already beginning the process of calming the set of feelings and fabrications that make up the emotion. As we observe the flow of thoughts, sensations, etc. that we identify as "anger" or "anxiety," we begin to let them slow down and settle. Then, finally, we can let it go.

Afterward, or if the emotion continues to arise, we can do what Thich Nhat Hanh calls "looking deeply" into the emotion. We ask ourselves, "What is this emotion?" and begin to look for its cause. Invariably, the cause originates in our view of the world—as an aspect of our view that is not in harmony with reality.

So in this final step, we again turn our attention to our thinking, analyzing and disputing the views that lead to unskillful emotions and actions. In REBT terminology, we might say we replace irrational beliefs with rational ones; in Buddhism we would say we cultivate views and intentions that align with the dharma.

However, we are not yet done with mindfulness: We continue to observe the unfolding of our thoughts, words and actions. And when we notice—nonjudgmentally and compassionately—that we have strayed, we patiently return ourselves to the path that leads to inner peace.

3 THE BRAHMA-VIHARAS

If you've read much about Buddhist meditation, you have probably heard about at least one of the Brahma-Viharas before. Many Western meditation teachers include Metta-Bhavana, Tonglen or some variation on these in their pantheon of practices. However, we're going to delve into these practices a little deeper than any you may have encountered elsewhere.

Some of the time, we'll be working in very traditional ways, but at the same time, we're also going to use the Brahma-Viharas as a framework for a other concepts, including Rational Buddhism, that aren't quite as traditional but that I have found fit in very well with this practice.

The Buddha pointed out that there are four specific mental states we should all cultivate, whether monks or householders. These are the Brahma-Viharas, which means "Divine Abodes" or Divine Abidings.

We'll start with *metta*, a Pali term usually translated as "goodwill" or lovingkindness. I'm not crazy about either of those, because they're just not very accurate, and the idea of "loving" can seem kind of "clingy," and that's not what we're after. I'll use the Pali word here.

Metta is a sincere desire for someone or some being, yourself included, to be happy—to be actualizing, to be free from animosity, free from stress, live peacefully. We will be using Metta-Bhavana, which means "cultivating metta," as the core of our meditation practice during this workshop.

The second of the Brahma-Viharas is *karuna*, or compassion, which is a pretty good translation for this one. Compassion is a desire for someone to be free from suffering. We will be cultivating it by using a Tibetan practice called Tonglen.

Mudita, the third Brahma-Vihara, is sometimes translated as gladness or sympathetic joy. Basically, this is unselfish gratitude for happiness and freedom from suffering. It's an antidote to jealousy or envy, because if you practice this, when something good happens to someone, you're happy for them.

We're going to look at gratitude while we're doing this, because this is the point where we can really come to realistically comprehend that metta and compassion are "flowing" both ways. As we practice mudita, we get to appreciate and enjoy (and recognize!) that we are recipients of compassion and kindness. We're going to do this primarily through use of Naikan.

Finally, we come to *upekkha*, or equanimity. This is the understanding that despite our wishes for happiness and freedom from suffering, life is often troublesome—a bumpy road. We'll talk about how to cultivate serenity despite that bumpiness, and learn that the opposite of attachment is acceptance.

Cultivating the Brahma-Viharas begins with metta—specifically with wanting happiness for yourself, and then extending that to include others. (Buddhaghosa, 1999)

Take a look at the Metta-Bhavana diagram that follows—it looks like a target. At the center of this target, you put yourself. In this particular meditation we're going to do, you start by wishing for happiness for yourself. After you've worked with that for a while, you're going to wish for happiness for a loved one, a good friend, a neutral person, someone "hostile," that you're having some conflict with, and finally all beings.

So I want you to take a moment now and put yourself in the center of that circle—whatever you feel like doing to symbolize you being there. And then choose people to put in all those other circles.

You're going to find other diagrams similar to this one in your workbook, by the way, and you're going to do something similar to this using the same people. So before you write anything down, think about the best people to consider in your contemplation.

The loved one should be alive in this kind of practice. This should also be someone you have no problem really wanting to be happy. Traditionally, you'd use your mother, but some people don't get along too well with their mother. That might be something to work on later, but for now, pick someone you feel really close to.

The friend, again, should be someone around whom you feel good. It doesn't have to be the one person in your life who's done the most for you or anything, but again, someone that you feel glad to be with when they're around.

The neutral person can be a challenge. Ideally, you want someone you know a little bit about, but don't feel one way or the other toward, and that can be hard. It might be someone you see at the grocery store regularly but haven't really gotten to know or someone like that. And don't be surprised if you find they're no longer neutral once you start working with them. That's part of the process.

Finally, you need someone with whom you're having some conflict—

someone you don't like very much or is otherwise difficult in some way. I would prefer you think of someone you have to deal with—a coworker, perhaps. If there's really no one, it can be a political figure or one of those cable news people you don't like or whatever. But it's better if it's someone you actually know.

Cultivating Metta for Yourself

We start out by cultivating metta for ourselves, in part because as the Buddha once pointed out, no one is more "dear" than oneself. But there are some things to think about as we get into this practice of cultivating metta for ourselves.

First, we're establishing the idea that happiness is good. We acknowledge that it's a goal we have, and that it's a good goal. We also acknowledge that the goal is attainable. If we don't have happiness now, we can work toward it.

That's kind of an important idea: that happiness comes from working for happiness. It doesn't just happen to us—fall on us from the heavens or something. It's a goal, and it's attainable through our own efforts. So when we think, "May I be happy," we're thinking, "May I do the things that cause happiness and abandon the things I've been doing that get in its way."

It can seem selfish to be spending that time thinking of our own happiness. Don't worry about that, though. It's hard to care for others when we're caught up in our own stuff and creating suffering for ourselves. If I'm creating suffering for myself, I'm probably visiting that on others in one way or another.

There's another thing to keep in mind, too. Happiness is unique in that when it's shared, it grows. That sounds counter-intuitive, but you'll probably find a lot of that sort of counter-intuitive stuff this weekend.

When we move on to metta for others, we need to keep a few things in mind. First, we wish for happiness for others, just as we wish for happiness for ourselves. However, we don't need to define what that means for them. Don't get caught up in "Okay, what's happiness for them? How do I contribute to it? What do I need to do?"

Some of those things might come up later as you're working on compassion and so on, but for now, this really isn't a problem-solving exercise. Your only objective is to cultivate metta for them—to wish for happiness for them, just like you wish for happiness for yourself: the difference being, of course, that this gives you a chance to consider the benefits of happiness and develop your intention to support it.

As you work through this, at some point, you may enter a jhana state—a state of absorption in the meditation object. If you haven't done much meditation, this may be a very new feeling for you. You may experience a *nimitta*, a sort of "sign" that you're reaching this state—a visual image, perhaps, or a sensation. Don't get caught up in this experience, but be aware of it. You can keep the feeling going by continuing to cultivate the meditation object.

Because you're doing some active thinking, this kind of jhana will probably feel different than the jhana you experience during a Vipassana retreat or whatever, but that's okay. Just try to keep it going.

As you move from one subject to another, you do what you need to do to break down the barriers, and then, once that's done, begin to pervade all directions with metta. The next work comes when you can't generate, or find it difficult to generate, metta for someone—or when you can't keep that jhana up as you transition to a particular person.

That's where you might start problem-solving: Where is the block coming from? Where's my resistance? And then take note of the thoughts that arise—mental notes, don't stop meditating to write stuff down—so we can work on those.

Metta-Bhavana: Cultivating Metta

Using the recorded meditation, try Metta-Bhavana meditation. There are also written instructions that you can refer to when you get ready to do it without the recording. As you work with this practice, consider the following:

Cultivating Metta for Yourself

- With this practice, we establish the idea that happiness is good. We acknowledge that it's a goal we have and that it's a good goal. We also acknowledge that the goal is attainable. If we don't have happiness now, we can work toward it.

- That's an important idea: Happiness comes from working for happiness. It doesn't just happen to us or fall on us from the sky. It's a goal, and it's attainable through our own efforts. So when we think, "May I be happy," we're thinking, "May I do the things that cause happiness and abandon the things I've been doing that get in its way."

- It's hard to care for others when we're caught up in our own stuff and creating suffering for ourselves. If I'm creating suffering for myself, I'm probably visiting that on others in one way or another.

- Happiness grows when it is shared.

Cultivating Metta for Others

- Wish for happiness for others, just as we wish for happiness for ourselves. We don't need to define what that means or should mean for them.

- Try to break down the barriers—to keep the metta "flowing" from one person to the next.

- When you encounter resistance, that's where you consider this: Where is the block coming from? Where's my resistance? Take note of the thoughts that arise to work on later.

Metta-Bhavana Preparation

1. Start with yourself, and your desire for happiness. List several ways your happiness is "blocked" now. During the meditation, you will resolve to work on these things. Other challenges may arise during the meditation, so don't worry about making the list exhaustive.
2. Next, write down the name of the person closest to you—your most beloved relative, friend, mentor, teacher, or whomever.
3. Now a friend—a good friend, preferably a spiritual friend.
4. In the next circle, list someone neutral. It might be a very casual acquaintance or someone you just see now and then.
5. Now list a difficult person, someone with whom you're having some sort of trouble or conflict.
6. All beings—what does that mean to you? What kinds of beings are there? Are there beings you have trouble with? Phobias? Make sure you work on that, too.

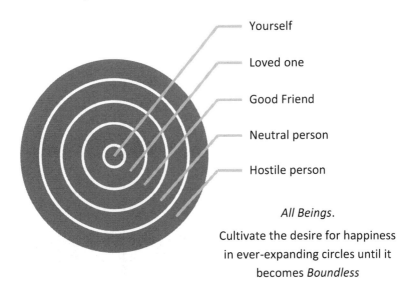

Yourself

Loved one

Good Friend

Neutral person

Hostile person

All Beings.
Cultivate the desire for happiness
in ever-expanding circles until it
becomes *Boundless*

Notes on Metta Meditation

1. Before you begin, note any problems getting in the way of your happiness now, anything you'd like to work on in meditation.

2. After the meditation, list any problems you had sending metta to yourself or others. Any other resistance encountered? Any other problems with meditation? Key insights? Any issues you'll want to investigate further?

Metta-Bhavana Instructions

1. Sit comfortably and spend a few moments just quietly observing the breath. Begin cultivating metta by directing a desire for happiness to yourself.

    There are a few traditional phrases: May I be happy. May I be free from animosity; may I be free from affliction and distress; may I live peacefully. Use those or choose others that reflect your desire for *true* happiness—happiness that is found in the present moment and that comes from within. Try to let the phrases emerge from your heart and "ride" on the breath.

    Be aware of any feelings that arise in connection with the phrases.

2. Next, direct metta toward a loved one—a parent or other benefactor who has cared for you, inspires you, or otherwise reminds you of your capacity to be loving, compassionate and aware. Envision that person or say their name silently to yourself; try to feel as if she or he is with you.

    Offer them the same wish for happiness you wished for yourself: May you be happy; may you be free from animosity; may you be free from affliction and distress; may you live peacefully. Don't try to define happiness for them, and there's no need to consider whether or not happiness is possible for them or get caught up in trying to decide how you could "make" them happy. Your only job is to wish them happiness.

3. Now expand your metta to include a good friend. You might consider envisioning metta radiating from you as a light, or feel it emerging from your heart. Be aware of any sensations or images that arise—any signs of jhana—and see if these signs remain constant as you change from one person to another.

4. Choose a neutral person -- someone you neither like nor dislike. All beings everywhere want to be happy. Even if you don't know this person well at all or understand their karma, you know they, like all beings, want happiness. Wish for them the happiness you wish for yourself.

5. Call to mind someone difficult and include them in your circle of metta. Be aware of any feelings that arise, and see any resistance as an opportunity to expand your ability to cultivate goodwill.

6. Send metta to all beings everywhere, without distinction: "May all beings be happy. May they be free from animosity. May they be free from affliction and distress. May they live peacefully."

7. Continue sending metta. You might send metta in the six directions—to the front, the right, the left, the back, above and below. Or to beings that walk or crawl, that fly, that burrow, that swim, etc.

4 WORKING WITH COMPASSION

As we learned earlier, cultivating the Brahma-Viharas starts with Metta, the wish for happiness. We could state metta as a *view*: All beings want happiness; happiness is attainable; and happiness is good for all beings.

From that view, we can cultivate the *intention* for compassion (karuna). In other words, I think happiness is good for all beings; therefore I will help them be free from suffering. To cultivate this intention, we're going to do a Tibetan practice called Tonglen, which means "sending and receiving." The idea is that we make ourselves willing to take on the suffering of others and exchange it for freedom from suffering—for relief of some kind.

The practice may seem a bit counter-intuitive at first. We don't want to suffer, of course, so we tend to reject the idea of "taking on for ourselves" someone's depression, anger or anxiety. In fact, some people meditate on breathing out negative emotions and breathing in peaceful ones, and that has its uses. But think about it this way—by taking on someone's depression, for example, you're not making yourself depressed. You're accepting that this kind of suffering exists, and you're receiving that realization with compassion—with the desire to help others (and yourself, in the process) transcend it.

We do this somewhat like we do metta—we start with one person and expand our circle of compassion. If we were just cultivating compassion the way it's done in Theravada Buddhism, we'd start with someone we want to help, and then send out a wish, "May you be free from suffering" to that person, and then our loved one, and so on.

However, we're doing this slightly different practice, so instead of "sending out," we're *taking in* first and then sending out.

You do this by breathing through the suffering you find. One way you can do this is to imagine suffering as black smoke (or if that bugs you, think of some other image) and then breathe it in. You can imagine it

30

transforming, in your heart, into white light, which you breathe out to the person for whom you're cultivating compassion.

There are different traditional instructions in where you start, by the way: You can either start with yourself or with someone who's suffering. I think it's good to practice it both ways. Here's an important point, though: Before we can have compassion for others, we need to accept and understand our own suffering, and then we can see it better in others.

So we're going to start by considering this word "suffering." The Buddha spelled out specific kinds of *dukkha* when he gave his first sermon and talked about the first of the Four Noble Truths:

- There is what's often called the "suffering of suffering"—birth, death, aging and illness.
- There is also suffering from circumstances, specifically separation from things we want and association with things we don't want.

In a nutshell, then, the five clinging aggregates (nama-rupa) are suffering: Life contains circumstances and situations that include adversities/afflictions and difficulties. However, how much stress and suffering we experience is mainly a product of the way we view those things. When we do Tonglen, we notice the situations that cause our suffering, we accept them, and then we work, with compassion, to abandon the ways we create more suffering.

When we start this, I think we can begin by cultivating acceptance of the suffering to which we are subject:

- Accepting this body is subject to aging, I'll abandon the ways I create more suffering so I can enjoy the present moment. In the meantime, I can compassionately accept myself when I suffer.
- Accepting this body is subject to disease, I'll abandon the ways I make my mind sick; in the meantime, I will compassionately accept myself when I suffer.
- Accepting this body is subject to death, I'll work harder to enjoy and make the most of the time I have; in the meantime, I will compassionately accept myself when I suffer.
- Accepting that circumstances will at times separate me from that which I love and enjoy, I will refrain from demanding life be otherwise.
- Accepting that life will sometimes ask me to associate with people and circumstances I don't like, I will refrain from demanding otherwise.

As you consider yourself, you imagine taking on and accepting different kinds of suffering, and then "send out" to yourself the ease you would like to experience. For example, say you're dealing with anger issues. You first accept that—you breathe in your angry feelings. And then you breathe it back to yourself with friendliness. You might breathe in anxiety, and then breathe out calmness.

So you see what you're doing? If we look at this in Rational Buddhism terms, we often see that people make themselves upset about being upset—they get mad at themselves for getting angry, for example. So you're accepting, "Okay, I have this karma, and I get angry." You breathe that in, but you also recognize that change is possible. So you breathe out non-anger.

Then you can move on to someone you want to help. This can be a "new" person, one that wasn't in your metta circles, but someone for whom it's fairly easy to arouse compassion.

When there is someone you want to help—like a survivor of a catastrophic natural disaster or someone in a war zone, for example—you can use that to cultivate compassion. You put them in the center and think, "This person has been reduced to misery. If only they could be freed from their suffering." Then you imagine you can breathe in that person's loneliness, grief, fear, and so on, and breathe out the relief.

Then arouse compassion for the dear person, the neutral person, hostile person, and finally all beings. Bring each to mind, and then imagine that you can breathe in or otherwise take on their suffering and breathe out or "send" them the alternative.

If someone is angry, you might send them friendship. If someone is anxious, imagine taking on their anxiety and sending them calmness. Take on depression and return joy, and so on.

You don't have to worry about how these people might be freed from suffering. You're just cultivating an intention, not problem-solving. You are, in a sense, taking on responsibility for the suffering in the world by recognizing your part in it and resolving to help with it, but you'll do that by reacting from a heart that has become more compassionate with this practice.

Tonglen: Cultivating Compassion

Using the recorded meditation and then on your own, cultivate compassion using Tonglen.

Summing up:

- Compassion for yourself
- And/or someone you want to help
- For your loved one
- For a good friend
- A neutral person
- A hostile person

- All beings—let your compassion grow boundless.

Tonglen Worksheet

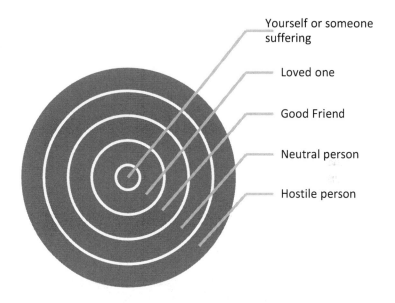

Yourself or someone suffering

Loved one

Good Friend

Neutral person

Hostile person

All beings: Cultivate compassion until it becomes boundless.

As you work on Tonglen, notice any difficulties that arise. During breaks between sittings, note the difficulties below for discussion and/or for Rational Buddhism work.

Sidebar: Compassion for difficult people—Casey Anthony

I live in Central Florida, where the Casey Anthony case was in the forefront of the community consciousness for several years and where the outcome of her trial was received with very strong emotions.

The Anthony case fueled a controversy rife with feelings of animosity, distrust and betrayal. However, rather than participate in the controversy over her guilt or innocence, perhaps we can use our feelings about such a tragedy as an opportunity for spiritual growth.

For a Buddhist, there are good religious reasons to abandon anger and cultivate kindness. However, there are also ample mental health-related incentives for transcending ill will and cultivating compassion—or at least what Albert Ellis termed "Unconditional Other-Acceptance"—for the Casey Anthonys of the world.

One of the sutras relates a conversation between the Buddha and his son, Rahula, a novice monk. The Buddha begins by asking his son, "What is a mirror for?" He goes on to explain that just as Rahula might use the reflection in a mirror to examine his face, he can use his awareness to reflect on his actions of body, speech and mind.

If, on such reflection, Rahula finds himself engaging in a harmful mental, verbal or physical act, he should abandon it. If he finds the action is helpful, he can continue it and even cultivate it. Like Rahula, we can use our minds to reflect on our acts of body, speech and mind and determine whether to abandon or cultivate them.

I suspect the typical thoughts that fueled animosity toward Anthony went something like this: "Casey Anthony did a terrible thing, so she is a terrible person who deserves damnation. Because she's so evil, she must be punished, and anyone who could have but didn't punish her is also a terrible person who deserves damnation."

As I mentioned above, such global self-rating is irrational and leads to stress and difficulty. Just as it is unskillful to rate one's ever-changing, indefinable "self," it is equally irrational to rate another's "self."

Let's use our mindfulness as a mirror to reflect on the most prominent of these other-rating views, "Because Casey Anthony did a terrible thing, she is a terrible person." We'll disregard the question of guilt—the irrationality (or ignorance, in Buddhist terms) has little to do with whether or not she is guilty, but whether or not her guilt makes her a "terrible person."

First, we can ask ourselves this question: Is there evidence to prove the belief that if someone does a bad thing, he or she is a bad person?

The answer is no—there is no evidence that Anthony is "bad" because she did a bad thing. A bad "person" could only do bad things, but we know all people do both good things and bad things, so there's no way this one terrible act makes her a terrible person.

In fact, we can now answer our second question, "Is there evidence that belief is false?" Anthony doubtless has some good qualities, so she can't possibly be a "bad person." Even if we could find very few good qualities in her, there is no reason she couldn't go on to do many good things in her lifetime.

Next, we can weigh the disadvantages of clinging to such beliefs and the advantages of relinquishing them. What happens if we continue believing that someone who does a bad thing is therefore a thoroughly bad, damnable person? We will probably continue to become enraged when people in the news—and in our personal lives—do bad things.

If we look closely into our hearts and minds, we discover that anger includes some pretty unpleasant sensations. We now see that these unpleasant feelings are the result of our mental processes, not the situation itself. If we can transcend the irrational mental formations at the source of our anger, we can end the suffering!

Freed from this filter of rage, we can now clearly see someone like Anthony as another being who, like us, our friends and our loved ones, is suffering the universal dukkha of aging, illness and impermanence. She has also lost her child. I've heard people discount that, using the perception that she may not exhibit adequate remorse as further evidence of her "terribleness." However, if this mother is not suffering from this loss, what kind of suffering must she have endured to get that way?

Cultivating compassion for the Casey Anthonys of the world won't cost you anything, but it will benefit you by helping you develop the capacity for compassion, which is a great strength. If you feel anger or other distress over such a situation, here are a few things to try:

(1) Work towards non-animosity by accepting that the other, like you, is an imperfect being struggling with the effects of past karma.

(2) Cultivate compassion for everyone involved in the case: Along with the subject herself and her family, this case involved judges, lawyers, law enforcement officers, jurors and their friends and families. Each of them have performed good actions and have good characteristics, and each have performed some unskillful actions and have negative characteristics. See if you can have compassion for the entire group.

(3) Cultivate some compassion for yourself. Recognize that you have caused yourself distress by generating feelings of anger or hopelessness, for example, and resolve to ease your own suffering without condemning yourself for it—you, too, inherited the effects of past karma.

(4) Rather than being resentful or feeling hopeless about an injustice, perhaps you can help prevent future similar situations by donating to or volunteering for community organizations that aid families in crisis, or ask your state representative to increase resources for agencies that assist children and families.

5 RATIONALITY, DHARMA & KARMA

Think a little bit about your goals for Buddhist practice—are you striving for Enlightenment? Trying to "reach" Nirvana? When we start practicing, we soon learn that Buddhist experience isn't as much transcendental as it is grounding. Yes, you will hopefully transcend some of your suffering, but you'll do that not by reaching some heavenly state so much as by learning how to experience "heaven" in day to day life.

I like what Kenneth Tanaka, a Jodo Shinshu minister and professor at the Institute of Buddhist Studies in Berkeley has to say about Buddhism in his book, *Ocean*: "The goal of Buddhism is to become more 'real' by becoming more aware of the true nature of oneself and of one's relationship to the world." (Tanaka, 1997)

When we look at our relationship to the world through the lens of Buddhist dharma, we start to see it more clearly; and when we see it more clearly, we cause ourselves less stress. There are very few things the Buddha said we "needed" to believe, but he did lay out a few key teachings, and we can apply these teachings to our work with the Brahma-Viharas.

Let's begin with the Four Seals of the Dharma:

1. Dukkha. All compounded things—that is, all things that arise from causes and conditions—are unsatisfactory.

2. Impermanence (Pali, *anicca*). All compounded things, that is, all things that arise due to causes and conditions, are impermanent and thus subject to change.

3. Not-self. (Pali, *anatta*) All compounded things are not self.

4. Nirvana (Pali, *nibbana*) Nirvana is peace.

Tanaka offers a clever mnemonic device for those in *Ocean*—he suggests using the word BIIG:

- Life is a *Bumpy* road.
- Life is *Impermanent.*
- Life is *Interdependent.*
- Life is fundamentally *Good.* (Tanaka, 1997)

"Life is a Bumpy road" represents the principle of dukkha: Disappointments and adversities are a normal part of human existence. Birth, death, aging, illness, being separated from loved ones and associating with that which we dislike—all those things happen to all of us. Rather than battling them, we can see them as steps toward enlightenment.

"Life is Impermanent" means nothing stays the same from one moment to the next—not our bodies, not other people, not conditions and not things. We can't expect our lives to stay the way they are. Things change over time, so when we're attaching our happiness to them—to accomplishments, to other people, to things and conditions, they never turn out the way we expect them to.

"Life is Interdependent," points to the same idea as the doctrine of Not-self. What we see as a "self" is very much connected to all kinds of other things, and it is part of an ongoing process of change. We think of our "self" as having discreet existence, but we're constantly changing and we are dependent on everything else around us.

The G stands for Good, as in "Life is fundamentally Good," which Tanaka equates to Nirvana—and Nirvana is peace, remember?

You might think the statement, "Nirvana is peace" isn't an instruction for practice, but what if you make it one? So *practice* Nirvana, right? So I think we can see this seal like this: There is a way to *practice* peace, and as a result, to experience more of it.

In many cases, that's going to mean letting go of something that seems to have a payoff—your anger, for example, or your "need" for approval, or your insistence that life be dukkha-free—and to understand that letting go of that is going to bring about a more peaceful life, a more peaceful mind.

Life is what you make it. And as you're looking at life in your Naikan practice, you may really start to see things differently. The more you cultivate awareness of reality and the fact that we're really supported by the world we live in, the better life looks.

There's another key Buddhist teaching, and that's the law of karma. Karma means "action." Earlier, I mentioned causes and conditions. There's a phrase that applies to people and beings that experience birth, suffering and death—"conditioned existence." By what are these things conditioned? By karma—by action.

There's a long-running dialogue in philosophy about nature and nurture—are people *born* good or evil? Are they *made* good or evil? Do they *choose* to be good or evil? In Buddhism, it's all of the above. Each of us is heir to our karma: We arise due to causes and conditions, and some of those causes and conditions include actions from our past lives—which we might perhaps interpret as social and genetic preconditioning. We're all born with some amount of hard-wiring in place in terms of our mental abilities and personality tendencies, and we're born into families and societies that encourage certain behaviors and discourage others.

So in a sense, both nature and nurture make us what we are. But then there's another factor, which is our present karma—our current willful actions. As we live, we create more karma. So we are influenced by our own karma and others' karma, and our karma influences the world around us.

There are a couple of important points to learn from that. First, we can change—we're not stuck with who we "are," because we "are" in a state of change, and our good actions can change us for the better. Also, when we consider others, we have to take into account that they, too, are the heirs to their karma.

Let's look at how those things relate to Rational Buddhism. Ellis pointed out three main Irrational Beliefs, which we can equate to ignorance-based Sankharas.

(1) "I must do perfectly well in important tasks and win the love and approval of people important to me."

(2) "Other people must treat me the way I want to be treated, and if they don't, they should be severely punished for their injustice and inconsiderateness."

(3) The conditions under which I live must allow me to get what I want with few hassles, and when they don't, it's too hard. (Ellis, 2001)

Let's look at this in more detail, and see what we come up with when we look at them in terms of the Buddhist teachings we've discussed here.

1. Because I strongly want to achieve and win significant others' approval, I absolutely must keep fulfilling these goals! I am a *good person* when I do good things, and I am a *bad person* when I do bad things.

- Doctrine of not-self: Where is this "I" that "must" do well? This "self" is a process of ever-changing circumstances, so it can never be totally bad.

- Karma: Since causes and conditions led to my birth as a fallible human, it is highly likely I'm going to make mistakes.

- Can you think of others?

2. Because I greatly prefer that people and conditions treat me considerately and fairly, they absolutely *must* do so. Others are good people when they do things I like, and they're bad people when they do things I don't like.

- Not-self: If I can't judge my own "self," it makes no sense to judge another's self.

- Karma: Others are also subject to causes and conditions, and it's unrealistic to insist they be otherwise.

- Other:

-

3. Because I greatly prefer that conditions treat me fairly, they absolutely must do so. If not, then this unfortunate condition is *completely* bad, is the end of the world, is totally devastating, is the worst possible thing that could happen, and makes my life totally devoid of possible pleasure.

- Dukkha: Life is a Bumpy Road, but it is ultimately Good, remember. Unpleasant conditions don't make the world "all bad."

- Impermanence: Things often don't work out as expected—so I might as well expect that!

- Other:

-

As you go through your disputing process on the Rational Buddhism Worksheets, you might take some of the things you learn and accumulate them as Rational Dharma Statements. There are a few we could glean from above, like "Life is a Bumpy road, but it's a Good one." Or "Things often don't work out as expected—so I might as well expect that!"

Rational Dharma Statements

Look over your ABC worksheets and jot down any Rational Dharma Statements that come to mind. You may want to incorporate them into your meditation later when we get to Equanimity or at the end when we meditate on all four Brahma-Viharas.

Rational Dharma Statements

6 WORKING WITH GRATITUDE

Before we get into the next of the Brahma-Viharas, mudita, we are going to prepare for it by adding another tool to our spiritual toolbox, Naikan.

Naikan is a Japanese word that translates roughly to "introspection." It refers to a system of self-reflection that was developed by a Jodo-Shinshu Buddhist, Yoshimoto Ishin, who began establishing Naikan centers in the 1950s.

Today, there are 40 Naikan centers in Japan, and the practice has spread through Europe. There is at least one center in the US, the ToDo Institute, which is headed up by Gregg Krech, whose work with Naikan inspired and provided the framework for the Naikan work you'll be doing in this program.

Naikan practice centers on asking ourselves three questions:

What have I received?

What have I given?

What troubles and difficulties have I caused?

During a retreat at a Naikan center, we would ask these questions about specific people who play important roles in our lives, giving us a way to reflect on our relationships with parents, relatives, teachers, children, partners and others. The process gives us a broader, more complete view of our lives by shifting our focus from ourselves to others and the world in which we live.

I first encountered Naikan in the mid-1980s when my fascination with Zen expanded to include an interest in Buddhism-influenced Japanese psychotherapies.

At the time, I was struggling with my feelings toward my father, who was alcohol-dependent, violent and abusive. I had refused to talk to my father for more than a decade, and since the birth of my son, he had been

41

trying to contact me more often. Understandably, he was experiencing mental pain over being shut completely off from his grandchild.

Using Naikan to reflect on my relationship with him (as well as my relationships with my mother and other people) helped me sort out some chaotic memories and attitudes, and thus eased a lot of psychological stress. It would be a stretch to say I "reconciled" with my father. However, I did begin communicating with him and let him into our lives, while wisely limiting the extent of that involvement.

For our purposes here, we won't be doing a highly detailed a person-by-person analysis of our relationships. However, we will use the same approach to gain a new, more realistic perspective on our relationship to the world in which we live, including the people around us.

When we examine our lives through the lens of Naikan, we start by looking at what we receive. In our first exercise, for example, we will look at what we have received during recent weeks.

For example, here's what I see if I spend just a few minutes looking back over the past two weeks: My wife proof-read and then improved the design for a newsletter I had created; I received about $80 in donations and a $250 honorarium; I got payment for a writing assignment and offered another; I was served a delicious meal at an Indian restaurant; I received two gift certificates from acquaintances; I got a free download of an Iggy Pop song; a real estate agent gave me a tour of a church that's for sale and information about it.

Notice, these are just simple descriptions of things that made my life a little better or easier. The other people's motives don't matter—the important thing is that I received the benefit of their efforts.

We tend to take these gifts for granted or to minimize their impact by feeling "entitled" to them. Consequently, we end up not noticing all the ways we are supported by our world. And this is unfortunate, because our experience of life and whether it is "good" or "bad" has very little to do with what happens to us and almost everything to do with where we put our attention.

There is a Japanese saying, "When you are enlightened, the grass and trees also become enlightened." This enlightenment of grass and trees does not happen because the grass and trees do some special practice that leads them toward Nirvana. Rather, their enlightenment happens as a consequence of our intention—we realize that we live in a compassionate world that supports us in countless ways.

What do we receive from grass and trees? We get shade from the sun and cooling cushioning for our feet, we get lovely green scenery to view, and we get oxygen, which is essential to our survival. We owe life itself to the grass and trees, and to countless other animate and inanimate beings and objects. Naikan helps us begin to recognize the extent of that truth.

When we start to list these things, we are often surprised by how much support we receive. When we look at the other side of the relationship—at what we give versus what troubles we cause—we often see an imbalance.

As we go through the process, a clearer picture of our life begins to emerge. We may realize how often we notice every detail of every inconvenience, every occasion in which someone gets in our way or fails to live up to our expectation while we overlook the ways in which we inconvenience others and create problems in our environment.

As we will see, Naikan reflection will enhance our understanding of the Brahma-Viharas by helping us see more clearly our relationships to those to whom we extend metta and compassion.

Naikan Exercises

Ex. One, Part One

Your first Naikan exercise is in two parts. First, simply consider the many things and types of support you have received from others recently. Spend 20-30 minutes on this exercise, reflecting on the past few weeks. What are the most important things you've received? Who made these things possible?

In the space below, make a list of the items you received, and for each, list some of the people that made them possible. As you go through this process, consider what your life would have been like without these gifts. Don't forget those things you might otherwise take for granted. There are no "small" gifts or "little things." And please remember, the other person's motivation doesn't matter—it's still a gift, even if you had to pay for it.

Item Received   **Person(s) who made it possible**

Ex. One, Part Two (Krech, 2002)

Spend several hours noticing the objects that make your life easier and consider the people and other beings that made each object possible. For example, consider this book: Who and what made this possible? Did you use a fork to eat a meal? A leash to walk your dog? Brew coffee in a pot?

1.   List as many objects as you can.

2.   Take a moment to acknowledge and mentally thank the people and other beings that made these objects possible—you can even thank the objects themselves for their support.

Naikan Exercise Two: Daily Naikan

Spend 20-30 minutes doing the daily Naikan reflection:

Daily Naikan Questions

1.   What did I receive from others today?

2.   What did I give to others today?

3.   What difficulties did I cause others today?

How to Report and Receive Naikan

If you are working through this Naikan section in a group, you may be asked to prepare a Naikan report, then present it and receive another's report. Following are instructions on how to give and receive Naikan reports and a form to use.

Giving a Naikan Report. Do not ask for or expect comments from your listener. Keep your report about five minutes in length. Your report should consist only of highlights, a general summary, or perhaps one or two aspects in detail. Don't cram or hurry your report. If five minutes goes by quickly and you didn't get to report all you had planned, that's okay—cut it short for our group's purposes. Remember you are on a group time schedule. You should plan beforehand what your main report will include and use secondary or back-up material only as time allows.

Receiving a Naikan Report. Be quiet; just listen. Make a conscious effort not to make any sounds. This is not an ordinary conversation. Sometimes we tend to make sounds to show we are being attentive; this is not necessary in listening to a Naikan report. You might also be tempted to make supportive remarks of understanding or approval, but these are not necessary; please avoid making any comments or sounds. Silently listen! Do give your full attention.

Naikan Report Procedure

Talkers will be in assigned seats. Listeners will then be seated. Introduce yourself unless you already know one another.

Listener: Hello; I'm _____

Talker: Hello, I am _____; I'd like to tell you my Naikan report.

Listener: It's my privilege to hear your report.

Gassho to each other.

(Talker gives his report)

Talker: That's my report; I appreciate you listening.

Listener: It was my honor.

Gassho to each other and wait for instructions.

7 MUDITA

In most instructions for cultivating the Brahma-Viharas, mudita gets a pretty short shrift. It's kind of a confusing concept, and it's sometimes a little difficult to see how it fits in. I think it's very helpful, though, to think of it in terms of appreciation or gratitude.

Appreciation for others plays an important role in cultivating metta and compassion. It can be helpful, if we're having difficulty, to consider the ways the objects of our goodwill contribute to our well-being. That's especially true when we get to mudita, which is directly related to gratitude in a more general way.

Mudita, like metta, doesn't translate really well. It's often described as sympathetic joy, which is pretty vague, or as appreciation. The idea, however, is that you're happy about another person's good fortune. In fact, the traditional phrase you use while contemplating it is "May all beings keep their good fortune." So on one level it's an antidote for jealousy and envy.

Metta is the desire for someone to be happy, right? Compassion is the intention to help other beings not to suffer. So mudita, in a sense, is where we acknowledge that we got what we want—I want you to be happy and not to suffer; I notice you're happy and not suffering. So I'm grateful for your happiness. Thus one could say that mudita is gratitude for the good fortune of others. Therefore along with the traditional cultivation of mudita we will continue to use gratitude in Naikan practice as a method of self-reflection.

When we begin practicing with the Brahma-Viharas, we are sending out—sending out metta, sending out compassion. Now, when we get to mudita, we get to acknowledge our receiving. We get to see now that life is a two-way process. We're sending out kindness and compassion, but we're also living in a kind and compassionate world if we just open our eyes to that reality. So this is a good place to see what we're receiving.

When we meditate on this, we can be a little creative if we want to. This may not be 100 percent traditional, but that's okay— we don't have to cling to tradition as long as our practice is authentic.

That said, Bhadantacariya Buddhagosa says to start this with the good friend, and I agree that's a good starting point. We're usually glad to see our friends, and we're usually happy for their success. So part of our process here is to be able to feel toward all beings as we would toward a good friend—we make everyone our friend.

We start with the boon companion, then the dear person, the neutral person, the hostile person , and finally all beings and ourselves. The idea is to break down the barriers between these different types of people in order to be impartially glad for everyone's happiness.

There are some interesting things we can do with this meditation. First, we can look at each of these people and think about them in terms of the three Naikan questions: What have I received from this person? What have I given them? And what trouble have I caused them? That is very likely to bring you to want them to have good fortune, and wanting to support them in that.

Then, to follow more along the lines of Ajahn Buddhaghosa's teaching, we can consider each of these people, thinking, "May you enjoy your good fortune." This gives us another interesting opportunity, too. Suppose you're considering your friend, and this friend is having some trouble? You were just thinking of him and wishing him freedom from trouble, and now you're thinking about his good fortune.

So what do you do?

Well, we can look at this in light of the seals of Buddhism— impermanence, for instance. You know these difficulties are impermanent, and that more good fortune will come his way. So he'll get through this.

Also, because you will also be switching from Rational Buddhism to Naikan for your main journaling activities, you've begun to see goodness where before you might have overlooked it. So you can still say, "May you enjoy your good fortune," because your friend has some good fortune now, and he'll have more good fortune later on down the road.

See the figure on the next page for the order of cultivation. As part of this process, notice the way you're supported by the world you live in. After going through the expanding circles of gratitude, wish the enjoyment of good fortune on behalf of all beings.

Mudita

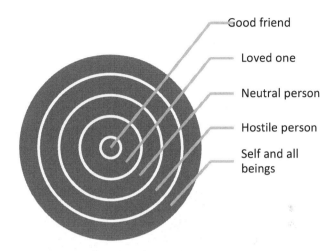

Good friend

Loved one

Neutral person

Hostile person

Self and all beings

Cultivating Mudita

Using the recorded guided meditation and insights that arise from your Naikan work, cultivate universal gratitude. Written instructions also follow.

Mudita Instructions

1. Begin with the Good Friend. Ask yourself the three Naikan questions: What have I received from this person? What have I given? What trouble have I caused? Then consider your friend's good fortune, too. Send this wish to your friend: "May you enjoy your good fortune."

2. Do this same procedure with your Loved One, Neutral Person and Hostile Person.

3. Finally, examine the ways you are supported by other beings, using the three questions, and then contemplate the thought, "May all beings enjoy their good fortune."

8 EQUANIMITY

The last of the four Brahma-Viharas, *upekkha* or equanimity, seems very different in some ways from the other three at first. Once you work with it for a while, however, you find it's essential to the practice. In fact, as you work with these on your own, you should always end with equanimity.

When you begin cultivating the Brahma-Viharas, you start with metta—the desire for happiness for yourself and others. From there, you go to karuna/compassion—the intention to help yourself and others be free from suffering. You acknowledge your appreciation for all beings and extend mudita—gladness—to them.

But what happens when there's not happiness? When there is suffering? When good fortune is lost? And what happens when I find it relatively easy to extend metta or compassion to a loved one, friend and even neutral person, but I hit a wall of resistance when I get to a difficult person?

That's where equanimity comes in.

Sometimes—despite my desire for your happiness, despite my intention to help you avoid suffering, despite my wish that you keep your good fortune—you will suffer, you have losses, and you're unhappy. Equanimity is the understanding that despite our good intentions, bad things happen—and we can accept these things, as they are. In other words, you're going to suffer sometimes. Do you want to only suffer? Or do you want to go ahead and be miserable while you're at it?

We hear a lot in Buddhist circles about not being attached. A lot of the time people think, "Well, Buddhists must be really detached, then." But that's not the case, either. Being detached means you don't care, and that doesn't make any sense: Buddhists also cultivate compassion, and how can you be compassionate and be detached? You can't.

I don't want you to suffer, but you suffer. I want you to be happy, but you're not. I want you to enjoy your good fortune, and you lose your job. If

I'm going to get all these things I don't want, and if I don't want to lose my mind, then what do I need? I need acceptance!

You know the story of Kisa Gotami and the Parable of the Mustard Seed. She didn't detach from the death of her child. Rather, she accepted—without liking it, without being "okay" with it, without becoming uncaring about it—that loss was part of life.

So that's what we do when we practice equanimity—we accept that things we don't like are going to happen and that we can experience losses without also losing our minds. We do this by acknowledging the role of karma in our lives. In fact, the traditional meditation on equanimity is a meditation on karma:

All beings are the owners of their karma, heirs to their karma.
Born of their karma, they are all related by karma.
All beings live supported by karma.
Whatever actions they do, good or evil, they will inherit the results.

I am the owner of my karma, heir to my karma.
Born of my karma, I am related to everything by karma
I live supported by my karma.
Whatever actions I do, good or evil, I will inherit the results.

I left a couple of unpopular words intact in this version of the equanimity cultivation: "good" and "evil." People tend not to like those words. I think we shy away from them because we associate them with moralistic attitudes or with the idea of supernatural evil.

Also, "good" and "bad" are relative terms. You could say that nothing is inherently good or bad; something is good or bad relative to our goals, or relative to what might help us or hinder us. So you will often see Buddhist writers substitute terms like skillful and unskillful, helpful and harmful, self-defeating and goal-supporting or whatever.

However, the words "good" and "evil" are pretty accurate if we realize we're talking about good versus evil views, intentions, and actions rather than good or evil people. We also don't mean good or evil in some absolutistic, other-ordained sense. An action isn't evil because someone says it's immoral—it's evil because if I do it, I will harm myself or others. Thus if I see an action is harmful, I should stop doing it.

You can evaluate your actions, but even if you see you've done a thoroughly evil act, that doesn't make you an "evil person." So go ahead and rate your acts, but don't rate yourself as a person.

And when you see that someone else is doing something you don't like, it's okay to not like it. But accept that they're acting according to the law of karma. If they're carrying around a lot of "evil" karma, they're going to do evil things. That doesn't make them evil people, though.

Here's another thing that happens when you cultivate equanimity—it tempers the other four Brahma-Viharas. You recognize the impermanence of the kind of happiness and joy we normally associate with love, compassion, and appreciation. So when cultivating equanimity, you see that those things eventually end—and so does misfortune, by the way.

So, if equanimity comes from acceptance, what are we accepting?

We can remember Tanaka's BIIG principle: Life is a Bumpy road; Life is Impermanent; Life is Interdependent; and even though things don't always go as we want, Life is ultimately Good.

Ellis also catalogued a list of things that we can work on accepting, and we can incorporate these into our meditations if we find them helpful:

Acceptance (Ellis, 2001)

• Accept yourself unconditionally, even though you have many failings.
• Unconditionally accept others with their shortcomings; accept the sinner, but not the sin.
• Accept the grim conditions of life when they cannot be changed.
• Accept dysfunctional feelings when you cannot change them.
• Accept present restrictions and pains that will produce future gains.
• Accept that your past cannot be changed, but your present reactions to it can be.
• Accept your biologically and socially learned limitations and don't demand they not exist.
• Accept your ultimate death, even though you would like to live forever.
• Accept your and others' fallibility and imperfection, and give to them and yourself the right to be wrong.
• Accept that you can change your thoughts, feelings and actions, but usually only with work and practice.
• Accept that few things are wholly good or bad—they are good or bad for a given time under certain conditions.
• Accept that you and others are often easily disturbable, and can act quite unreasonably and upsettingly. Accept others with their self-upsetting.

Equanimity Meditation

Begin this meditation by calling to mind the neutral person; envision him or her and acknowledge they are the owner of their karma. You can memorize the "All beings are the owners of their karma" chant above, or you can try to condense that into a few statements that sum it up for you.

Once you've established equanimity in jhana, try to maintain it as you work your way through your loved one, friend, hostile person, all beings, and yourself.

As you go through this process, you can remind yourself of the advantages of having a mind that is balanced and at peace. You can feel yourself sitting amid all this action—all these causes and conditions coming together and falling apart—and remaining peaceful.

Meditating on equanimity is a good place to recap any Rational Dharma Statements. You can use the acceptance list above to inspire some, if you like, and of course feel free to include any you already have. Note any obstacles that arise during your meditation, and try analyzing them on one of the remaining ABC Worksheets.

Cultivating Equanimity

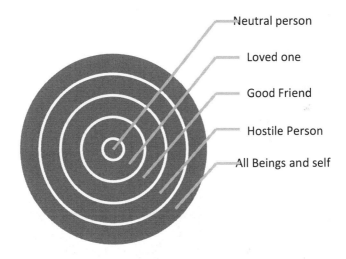

9 PUTTING IT ALL TOGETHER

By now, you should be breaking down the walls between yourself and the people you love, like, are neutral toward and with whom you have conflicts. At some point, you're going to find it fairly easy to enter into jhana with each of them. You'll get absorbed into these sensations and thoughts without losing concentration.

So when putting all the Brahma-Viharas into once meditation, start with metta for yourself and enter into jhana; move to the loved one without losing that jhana; then to the good friend and so on through the hostile person and then all beings, maintaining the absorption the whole time. Then you move on to compassion, mudita, and equanimity.

However, there is no one "right" way to cultivate the Brahma-Viharas; I have listed a few different approaches below. Use your common sense, good judgment and your own mindfulness and wisdom.

However, it's always advisable to finish with equanimity and acknowledge the effect of karma. Try to make sure you stick with that long enough to actually arouse some equanimity. Compassion and metta are great, but you need that reminder that both happiness and suffering are compounded things and therefore are impermanent.

Practice: Cultivating the Brahma-Viharas

Use the guided meditation to cultivate the Brahama-Viharas, but continue exploring ways to do it on your own using the guidelines above or following guidelines:

1.   Cultivate each in turn. Use the thought, "May I be happy" and the other phrases to generate the feeling —the sensation—that goes along with metta until you become absorbed into it, entering into jhana with metta as the object. Move to the loved one without losing that jhana; then to the good friend and so on through the hostile person and then all beings,

maintaining that absorption the whole time. Once you have "broken down the walls," you can transition from one to another without losing the jhana associated with metta.

Then you move on to compassion. See for yourself if it works better for you to start with yourself or someone you want to help. Go on to the loved one, the friend, the neutral person, the hostile person and finally all beings.

Move on to mudita, this time starting with your friend. Get the gladness going and keep it going—you can use the Naikan questions if you need to, and then just keep saying, "May you keep your good fortune" as you move from one person to another. Take a moment to be thankful in general for the support you receive from all beings.

Move on to equanimity. Remember to start with the neutral person here and then go to the loved one, friend, hostile person and finally all beings and yourself. Ideally, you will memorize the whole saying on karma, but you can come up with a statement that sums it up for you. You might also recite your Rational Dharma Statements to yourself during this portion of the meditation.

2.   Contemplate all four, but emphasize one. Contemplate all four Brahma-Viharas going straight to "all beings," but emphasize one of them in depth. You can do that based on what you feel you need to work on, or rotate from one day to the next.

3.   Start with Metta and then work with whatever arises. This is probably the most common way to do this—you simply start cultivating metta and go from there, based on whatever comes up. You might be sending metta, for example, and find that someone arouses compassion. Another person might have had some luck or something, so share enjoyment of their good fortune.

4.   Generate the Brahma-Viharas for all beings. Use this as a guide, and stick with each until you feel absorbed into each, and then move on to the next:

Metta:
May I be happy.
May I be free from animosity.
May I be free from stress and affliction.
May I live peacefully.

May all beings be happy.
May all beings be free from animosity.
May all beings be free from stress and affliction.
May all beings live peacefully.

Karuna
May all beings be freed from stress and suffering.

Mudita

May all beings enjoy their good fortune.

Upekkha

All beings are the owners of their karma, heirs to their karma.
Born of their karma, they are all related by karma.

All beings live supported by karma.
Whatever actions they do, good or evil, they will inherit the results.

10 ADDITIONAL RESOURCES

Opening Service for Rational Buddhism retreats and workshops

Incense Dedication

The fragrance of this incense invites the awakened mind to be truly present with us now.

The fragrance of this incense fills our room, protects and guards our minds from wrong thinking.

The fragrance of this incense unites us.

With precepts, concentration, and insight

we offer it for all in Oneness.

Homage to the Buddha

Namo tassa bhagavato arahato samma –sambuddhasa (three times)

(Homage to the blessed one, the pure one, the rightly self-awakened one.)

Three Treasures Reading: Going for Refuge

Sensei: I go to the Buddha for guidance.

ALL: I shall become one with the Buddha. I resolve that I shall each day follow the Way of Life he laid down for us to walk and awaken to his supreme wisdom.

Sensei: I go to the Dharma for guidance.

ALL: I shall become one with the Dharma. The gates of Dharma are manifold; I vow to enter them all. The goal of wisdom is ever beyond; I shall attain it.

Sensei: I go to the Sangha for guidance.

ALL: I shall become one with the Sangha. In the spirit of universal fellowship and as a member of the Sangha, I pledge myself to strive for the enlightenment of all beings.

Taking the Precepts

Sensei: Do you undertake the training precept not to kill or harm other beings?

Participants: I vow to respect all life as sacred. I vow to protect all life and prevent unnecessary destruction of life. I vow to not physically or verbally attack another person, animal or living thing.

Sensei: Do you undertake the training precept not to take what isn't freely given?

Participants: I vow to respect that which belongs to others and to take nothing that is not freely given. All that is given to me I vow to honor and reciprocate.

Sensei: Do you undertake the training precept not to abuse or exploit others?

Participants: I vow to respect my body and the bodies of others. I vow to be conscious of my actions toward self and others. I vow to become aware of the suffering that may be caused when others are involved in satisfying my wishes. I vow to treat all children with love, patience, and gentleness.

Sensei: Do you undertake the training precept to use speech carefully?

Participants: I vow to be truthful and to speak out about injustice. I vow to respect that which another speaks to me and to honor what is shared in confidence. I vow to be sincere and to keep commitments.

Sensei: Do you undertake the training precept not to cloud your mind?

Participants: I vow to honor the opportunity of being born and to develop the consciousness of my being. In keeping with this vow, I vow to live with mindfulness and to abstain from that which numbs me to the suffering of myself and others. I vow to cultivate a life of serenity and through my actions be an example for others to discover their own life of liberation and tranquility.

Closing Service

Homage to the Buddha

Namo tassa bhagavato arahato samma –sambuddhasa (three times)

Sensei:

The Dharma is deep and lovely.
We now have a chance to see it, to study it, and to practice it.
We vow to realize its true meaning

Metta Sutra

One skilled in goodness,
Who has seen the path to peace
Should live this way:

Let them be able and honest,
Easy to instruct and gentle in speech,
Humble and not conceited,
Contented and easily satisfied,
Living simply with modest duties.
Peaceful and calm; wise and skillful,
Never proud nor greedy.
Let them not do the slightest thing
The wise would later reprove.

Let them wish:
In gladness and in safety,
May all beings be at ease.

Whatever living beings there may be;
Whether they are weak or strong, omitting none,
The great or the mighty, medium, short or small,
The seen and the unseen,
Those living near and far away,
Those born and seeking birth—
May all beings be at ease!

Let none deceive another,
Or despise any being in any state.
Let none through anger or ill-will
Wish harm upon another.

Even as a mother protects with her life
Her child, her only child,
So with a boundless heart
Should one cherish all living beings;
Radiating kindness over the entire world:
Spreading upward to the skies,

And downward to the depths;
Outwards and unbounded,
Freed from hatred and ill-will.
Whether standing or walking, seated or lying down
Always alert, one should sustain this recollection.
This is said to be the divine abiding.

Not clinging to wrong views,
But virtuous and with clear vision,
Freed from sensual desires,
Never again will such a one
Return to the womb.

Closing Benediction

Sensei: We surround all people and all forms of life with love and
compassion. Particularly do we send forth loving thoughts to those in
suffering and sorrow, to all those in doubt and ignorance, and to all who
are striving to attain truth.

All: May the Infinite Light of Wisdom and Compassion so shine within us
that the errors and vanities of self may be dispelled; so shall we
understand the changing nature of existence and awaken into spiritual
peace.

Sensei: To all Enlightened Ones...

All: ...who are present in their teachings, we pledge our loyalty and
devotion. We dedicate our lives to the way of life they have laid down
for us to walk. We resolve to follow their example and labor earnestly
for the enlightenment and welfare of all beings.

Sharing Blessings

[Sabbe satta] sada hontu
Avera sukha jivino
Kataṃ puñña phalaṃ mayhaṃ
Sabbe bhaghi bhavantu te.

May all beings always live happily,
Free from animosity.
May all share in the blessings
Springing from the good we have done.

Continuing your practice.

When we work through the processes explained in this book in retreats and workshops, most people tell us that while Rational Buddhism, the Brahma-Viharas meditations and Naikan exercises were all helpful, one of them "clicked" more than the others.

You probably feel similarly—either doing ABC spreadsheets, cultivating these states of mind or exploring your life through gratitude seemed to especially resonate for you. Good! Keep working with it!

Perhaps you've read this book and done the exercises on your own, during the course of a several-week workshop or a several-day retreat. In any case, don't think you've gotten everything you can out of this material. If you make daily Naikan journaling, meditation or Rational Buddhism self-examination a regular part of your life, you will continue to awaken to a freer and deeper spirituality.

I suggest you not focus entirely on the one thing you "like," at least for a while. You may find that as you explore the other practices, different ones will seem more relevant at different times, either because your situation changes, your experience of your world evolves, or you come to understand a practice more deeply.

Also, you may occasionally have a dramatic, earth-shaking epiphany. More often, however, you will find your awakenings have been more subtle. You may realize one day that, without even noticing it, you've become less angry or less anxious.

Of course, this book isn't the be-all and end-all of this self-exploration, either. There are a number of great resources that can help you move forward in your practice, such as Gregg Krech's book on Naikan and the ToDo Institute's Naikan retreats and online courses.

Albert Ellis wrote prolifically on the subject of applying the ABCs to daily living, and there is a seemingly infinite number of books dealing with Buddhism and meditation available.

If possible, I strongly recommend getting involved with a good spiritual community, one with a knowledgeable teacher. There's nothing wrong with reading books by famous Buddhist writers and going to their retreats. Over the long run, however, you'll benefit more from being involved with a local community and working with a teacher who can who can take the time to get to know you personally.

Following is a list of resources and suggested readings.

Suggested books and online materials

REBT: Albert Ellis, Ph.D., was a very prolific writer, and he often put his theory into a form suitable for self-support. Many of his titles are available at Amazon.com and at the Albert Ellis Institute (www.rebt.org) . Consider beginning with *How to Stubbornly Refuse to Make Yourself Miserable About*

Anything, Yes Anything!, How to Make Yourself Happy and Remarkably Less Disturbable, or *Feeling Better, Getting Better, Staying Better.*

Also, the REBT Network has a good selection of online resources, including apps for using REBT for self-help. Visit their website at www.rebtnetwork.org.

The Brahma-Viharas: The *Visuddhimagga* (Path of Purification) gives detailed instructions on traditional methods of working with the Brahma-Viharas. It is available online in its entirety at Access to Insight, www.accesstoinsight.org.

Naikan: Visit the ToDo Institute online at www.todoinstitute.org. The institute has books like Gregg Krech's excellent *Naikan: Gratitude, Grace and the Japanese Art of Self-Reflection* as well as online and resident programs in Naikan and other forms of Japanese Psychotherapy and personal development.

Practice Communities

Bright Dawn Center for Oneness Buddhism: Bright Dawn's online sangha offers online dharma talks via "Live Dharma Sunday," a "Dharma-to-Go" program where visitors can ask for input from Bright Dawn senseis, as well as books and other resources. brightdawnsangha.ning.com

Volusia Buddhist Fellowship: Volusia Buddhist Fellowship meets every week at the First Unitarian Universalist Church in DeLand and holds other meetings and events elsewhere from time to time. There are some meditation instructions as well as listings of meetings and upcoming events at our website, www.volusiabuddhist.org.

Works Cited

Buddhaghosa, Bhadantacariya. (1999). *Visuddhimagga: The Path of Purification.* (B. Nanamoli, Trans.) Onalaska, Washington: Pariyatti Publishing.

Ellis, A. (2001). *Overcoming Destructive Beliefs, Feelings and Behaviors.* Amherst, New York: Prometheus Books.

Krech, G. (2002). *Naikan: Gratitude, Grace and the Japanese Art of Self-Reflection.* Berkeley, California: Stone Bridge Press.

Nhat Hanh, T. (1991). *Peace is Every Step.* New York: One Spirit.

Stahl, B. a. (2010). *A Mindfulness-Based Stress Reduction Workbook.*

Oakland, California: New Harbinger Publications, Inc.

Tanaka, K. (1997). *Ocean.* Berekeley, California: Wisdom Ocean Publications.

The Dhammayut Order in the United States of America. (1994). *A Chanting Guide.* Ontario, California: Dhammayut Order in the USA.

ABOUT THE AUTHOR

Sensei Morris Sekiyo Sullivan is the primary dharma teacher at Volusia Buddhist Fellowship in DeLand, Florida, and meets weekly with about 30 Buddhist inmates at Tomoka Correctional Institution.

He received his Sensei credential in 2010 from Bright Dawn Center for Oneness Buddhism, a non-sectarian tradition based on Japanese Mahayana Buddhism. In 2013, he received dharma transmission and the dharma name Pháp Hương Nhất from Ven. Khai Thien, abbot of White Sands Buddhist Center, making him a 42nd generation lineage holder in the Lam Te Chuc Thanh Dharma Lineage of Rinzai Zen.

Before his involvement with Bright Dawn, Rev. Sullivan ordained as a Theravada monk and studied Vipassana meditation with Than Chaokhun Sunan Phra Vijitrdhammapani, the abbot of Wat Florida Dhammaram in Kissimmee,

Rev. Sullivan's interest in Buddhism and Eastern Religion began in the 1960s while he was a teenager living in Texas. In the mid-1970s, he began reading about Zen Buddhism while studying philosophy and religion at a community college in Central Florida. His first formal Buddhist practice began around 1990, when a Unitarian minister in Orlando founded a meditation group modeled after Thich Nhat Hanh's Order of Interbeing practice tradition.

Along the way, Rev. Sullivan also explored Tibetan practices like Tonglen and Lojong. While leading meetings of a recovery group that used Rational-Emotive Behavior Therapy (REBT) as an alternative to 12-Step self-support, he became fascinated with the similarities between Albert Ellis' theories about psychology and the Buddha's teachings.

Besides this work, the former journalist and freelance writer authored *Wisdom; Compassion; Serenity: First Steps on the Buddhist Path* and co-authored *The Path of the Buddha*, a collaboration with photographer Gary Monroe (*The Highwaymen: Florida's African-American Landscape Painters*) about the Buddhist pilgrimage sites in northern India and Nepal.

Made in the USA
Columbia, SC
09 March 2021

34124782R00041